Loving Soulfully

The Key To Rising In Love

Written, Photographed & Designed by Rohit Juneja

Bodyscape Photographs by Ankha Desh

(pages 32, 60, 66, 68, 74, 76, 84, 96, 103, 112, 116, 124)

Edited by Karen E. Kelsay

Creative Design: Saima Farrukh (Kainat Zahra)

Paperback 2nd Edition in B&W, August 2016. ISBN-13: 9780988398955

Paperback 1st Edition in Color, January 2013. ISBN-13: 9780988398917

Available in E-Book version on Amazon.com and Apple iBook Store

Additional Books by Rohit Juneja:

God You Sexy Devil (Amazon.com)

Preface

"Loving Soulfully" began as a few verses written to someone I loved dearly. When we parted ways my heart was devastated. I was lost, confused and could make no sense of what had happened. In despair I reached out to the Universe or God, pleading for guidance and clarity. The sky didn't open and the seas didn't part but over the next year, the little whispers of my "inner voice" spoke to me. The insights came when I least expected them, as I walked, as I was speaking with a friend or as I commented on posts in Facebook.

Then life took a turn for the worse, I found myself in a financial dilemma. My savings had been depleted, my clients vanished and I couldn't afford even the basics of life. I had a choice: to pursue money or follow my inspiration. I chose the latter. For the next 3 months I lived in a tent, where I compiled all the messages that I had been recieving and organized them into this book.

One day as I was putting it togther, in a flash of inspiration, I saw an image in my mind of these words adorned with photographs. I had never done this kind of photography. I decided to experiment and try it out.

This entire body of work came through me and not from me. It was divinely inspired.

Many of the photographs are designed to evoke a meditative state similar to that which I experienced when I was writing. I invite you to consider the unusual message of "Loving Soulfully." It blends the essence of Bhakti and Sufi poetry with modern spiritual thinking. In doing so it resolves many of our age old love wounds and opens the doors to a new paradigm of Love.

In my journey of seeking, receiving and applying these teachings I experienced everything that I have written in this book. I trust that it will bring to you the wondrous gifts I received.

With Love,

Rohit

Table Of Contents

Acknowledgements

I am deeply grateful to:

My parents Promila and Prakash, as well as my daughter Govindi, for all their love and support.

Winnie, Anu, Elisa, Noopur, Kainat for teaching me the ways of love. Without their enormous contribution to my life none of this would have been possible.

Special thanks to:

Karen, my editor, who made the process of editing an uplifting, co-creative and joyous process.

Ankha Desh for her beautiful 'Bodyscape' photography as well as her support, suggestions and endless encouragement!

Kainat for her tremendous, unwavering support and commitment to this work.

Asudharam who helped me to connect with God and listen to my "inner voice."

Above all I am deeply grateful to Source, the Universe, God for guiding and using me to create this beautiful book. In all humility I surrender it back to you, that it may find those who will be inspired by its message.

Chapter 1: I Am Love

Chapter 1: I Am Love

The tears of yesterdays have dried after their incessant downpour;
The rhythm of my breathing is all that remains of the life I once had.

Breath carries me deep within myself.
I find peace but feel disturbed.
I find hope but feel disillusioned.
I feel saddened and broken beyond repair.

I bring my tale of sadness, loss and pain to the shore of aloneness.
I call out to endless waters and vacant skies,
"What shall I do, where shall I go, who will love me now?"

An inner voice beckons, "Let go of everything and come home."
I protest, "I do not want to give up and die!"
She replies, "Death is an illusion! You who are deathless
Must die every moment to be reborn into timelessness."

I trust Her words.

A vast emptiness stretches around me in all directions.

Fearful, I dive into its endless depths,

Its terrible black waters.

Deep within myself I know that I will find my way

Through this sea of infinite emptiness.

The Void engulfs me within its mysterious waves,

Its warm, soothing, liquid caresses.

Fear of the unknown,

Regret at my foolishness,

Rush in to overwhelm me.

I surrender to the nothingness; I lose myself.

I allow it to carry me, create me, infuse me.

I become nothing: empty -- open -- free.

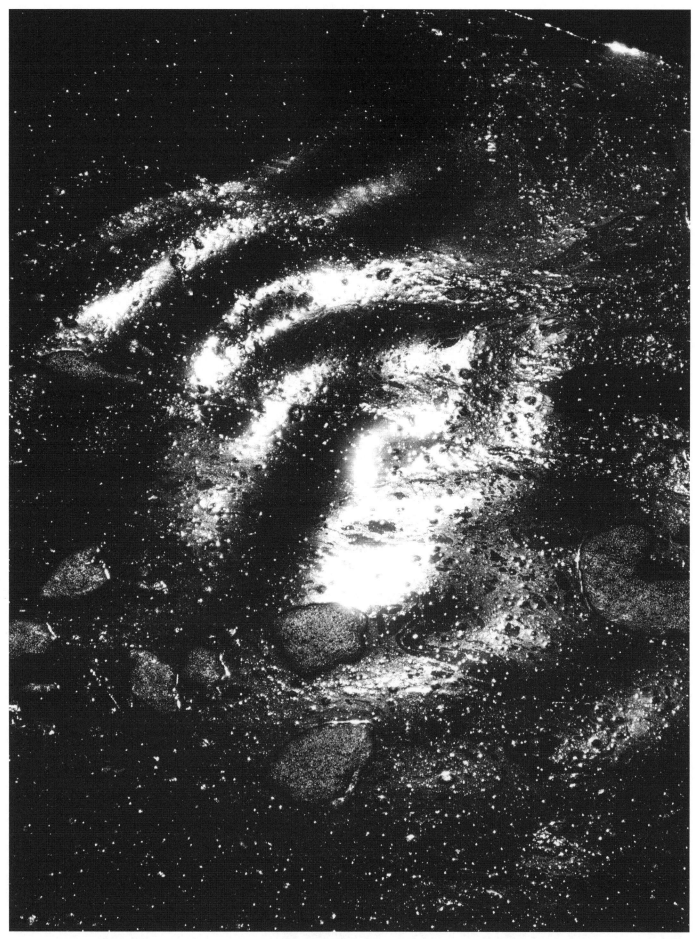

Arms open to embrace me.

Her voice soothes me with its tender love:

"I am here for you.

I honor you for trusting, surrendering,

And allowing me to care for you."

Her gentleness revives my soul.

Life returns, hope awakens, and

I whisper, "I am home at last!

I feel more alive than ever."

Loving Soulfully

A deep peace floods the depths of my being.

Like the morning sun,
Love awakens in my heart.

Splashing my soul with Her colors,
Painting its timeless skies
With Her dazzling hues;
Inviting me to awaken
To this blessed gift of Divine Love.

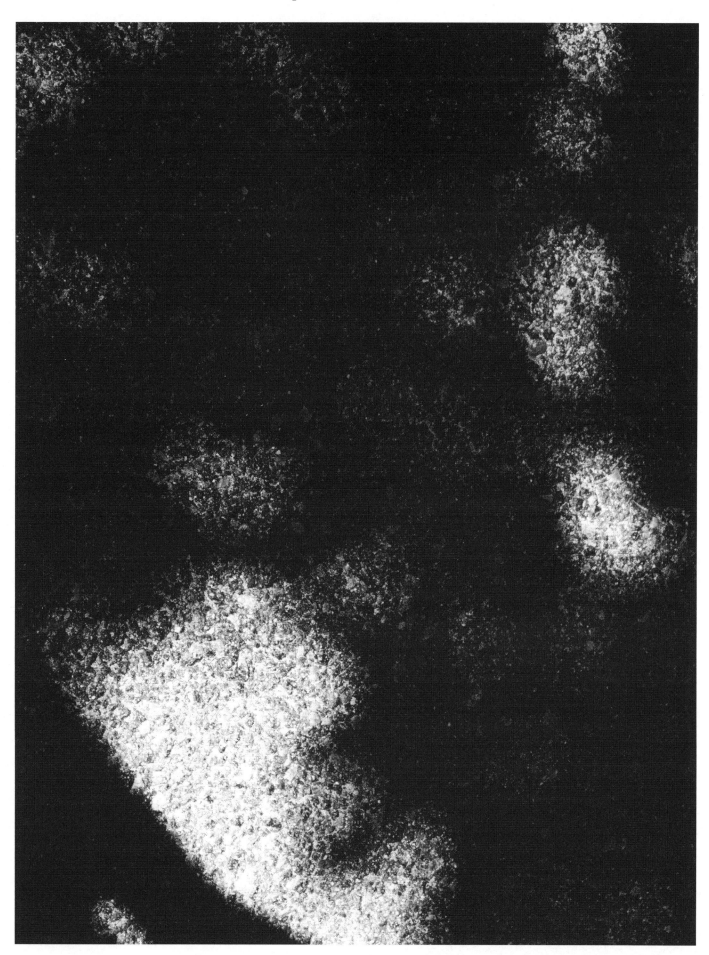

The inner voice continues,

"Broken and tormented you come to me asking,

'Where is love, why am I alone, why does love torture me?'

Look now at your creation:

Do you find beauty, peace, joy, freedom, hope and love; or

Do you see battlefields littered with pain, hurt, anger, sadness and fear?

You have turned to people and things to meet your needs

For love, happiness, pleasure and security.

You have chased money, fame and power.

You have believed in science, religion and politicians.

You have worked hard, played hard and tried every thrill imaginable.

Yet no matter what you believed or did,

No matter how much or how little you have had,

Your thirst was never quenched.

You have been chasing shadows life after life."

"What you long for cannot be found outside of you.

The treasure you seek,

The answer to all of your troubles,

Lies freely, abundantly and endlessly within you!

Within you lies your Self, your soul, your essence.

Therein shall you find the fulfillment of all your desires;

Therein shall you find unlimited, everlasting love, peace, joy and wisdom.

What you do not see within will be invisible in your world,

And what you see within you will find everywhere."

"Love not another unless you have first learned to love your Self.

Seek not the one who will fulfill and love you like no other.

The One you seek lies within!"

"You are the one true love for which you long.

You are the one you desire.

You are the one who will fulfill you.

You are the lover and the beloved.

You are the source of all your suffering and joy.

You are the destroyer and creator of your world.

You are the God of your life, and everything revolves around you.

You are full of endless possibilities and wondrous miracles."

Loving Soulfully

"No one can open the doors to the paradise within, except you.

No one can free you from the prison of existence, except you.

No one can save you, liberate you, or enlighten you, except you.

No one can give you what you need unless you give it to your self first."

"The Soul of Love unfolds

When you adore, nurture and embrace your Self unconditionally;

When you romance your Self tenderly, passionately and sensually.

Within your Self you will find the most intoxicating elixir;

The secret to unlimited, unending, Soulful Love;

The key to fulfilling your deepest desire and longing.

Your Self knows how to love you the way no one ever will.

Your Self will never betray you or leave you.

Your Self is the only thing that is truly yours, now and for eternity."

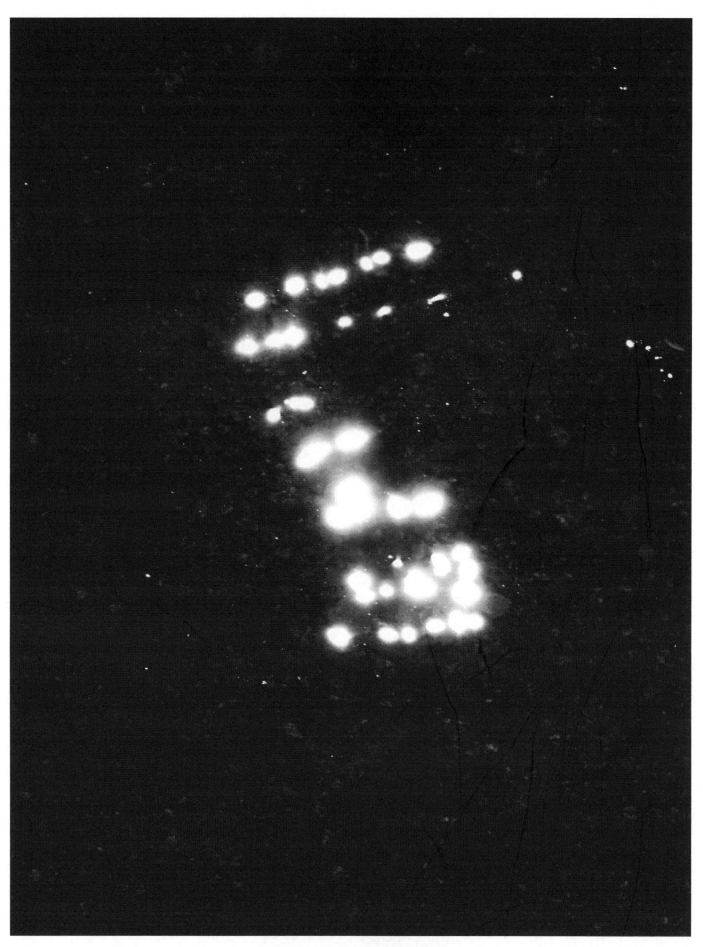

"Unleash your inner power by embracing your Self, as you are.

See how breathtakingly beautiful you are!

Hear how brilliant, wise and talented you are!

Know that you are perfect, with all of your flaws and imperfections!

You are the perfection that you have been seeking!

Live true to your Soul, your Higher Self,

Align with its wisdom,

And let it be your guiding light."

Chapter 2: Soul of Love

I ask,

"Will I ever find someone

Who will nurture, care for and love me;

Who will complete me, adore me, and make me feel special;

Who I can call my own and be with forever?

Is it true that one day I will meet my ideal lover and soul mate?

I wonder, is the ideal of 'romantic love' true?

I want to know what love is!

I want to experience true love!

I have tried and failed.

Will you show me the way?"

The inner voice replies:

"The mythology of 'romantic love' is a
Mentally concocted,
Religiously manipulated,
Socially conditioned,
Media enhanced delusion
That has nothing to do with true Love.

The knight in shining armor will never save you.
The perfect mate will never complete you.
The 'happily ever after' fairy tale ending will never come to pass.

If you really want to fulfill your soul's yearning
For undying romance, passion and true Love;
If you really want to free yourself from these grand illusions
That have birthed deep pain, disappointment and betrayal --
Then come with me on a journey into the heart and Soul of Love."

"Know this now and forever:

Love never hurts.

Love never betrays.

Love never dies!

Love is always with you.

Love is who you are!

The only thing hurting you is you!"

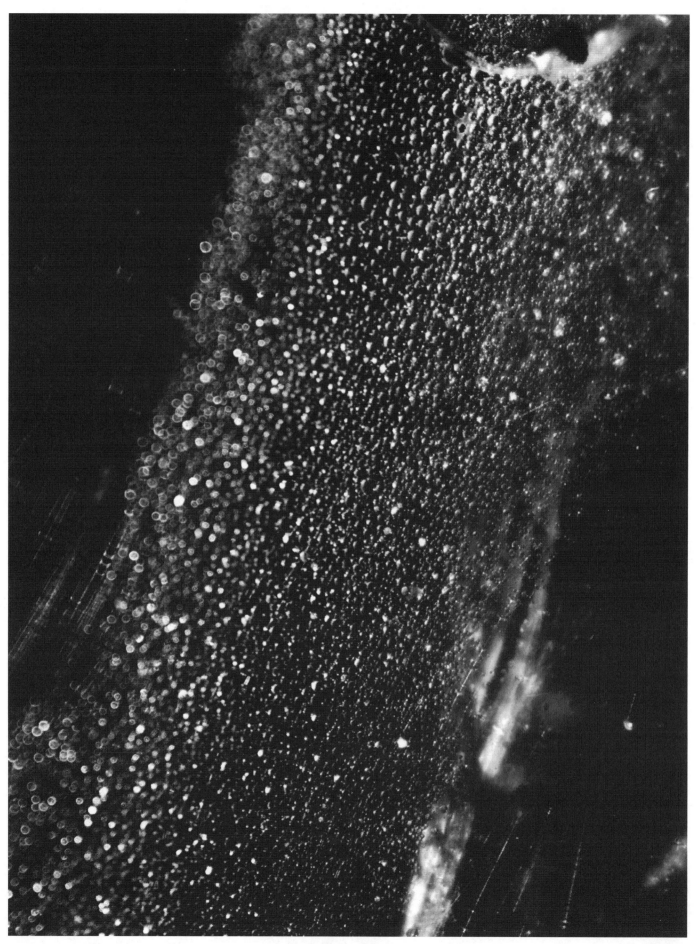

"When you think of your lover

As the one true love

Who will complete you, save you and fulfill your needs,

Then you set yourself up for failure.

Your vision is sweet and romantic,

But no person can ever live up to it.

Your expectations seem sensible,

But they are unrealistic and will trap you in a web of emotions.

Do not blame your lovers

For having disappointed, hurt and betrayed you.

The root cause of all your tragic love stories is this

Egoic ideal of romantic love."

"You think you need love

Because life without it feels hollow and empty.

You think love is lacking

Because it is closely guarded and given conditionally.

You struggle to find love and then struggle to hold on to it.

When your lover leaves you feel brokenhearted and are afraid to love again.

This experience born of lack and fear is not Love.

It is an unconsciously created simulation of love."

"Break the chains of romantic love
That have caused infinite loneliness, disappointment and pain!

Step out of your mind,
And let go of your sad stories
Of hurt and betrayal!

In holding them you only punish yourself
And re-create that which you do not want."

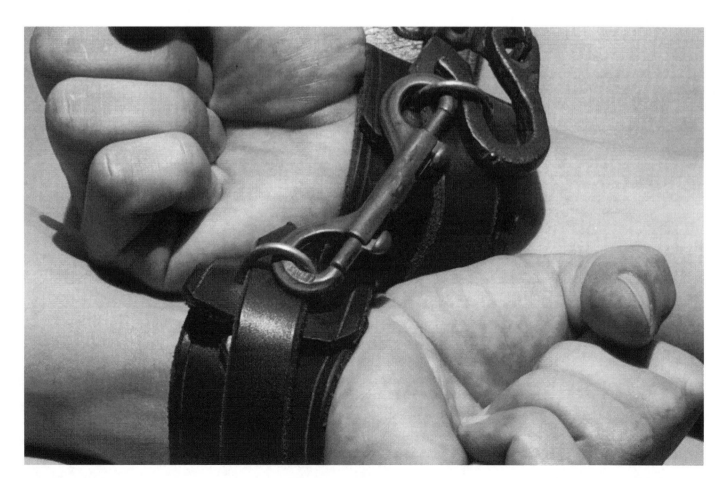

"Love lies at your core.
Your soul longs to love and be loved.

You have felt Love many times but
Have had no idea how to honor it.

You want to find your soul mate, but
Unless you connect with your soul
How will you recognize another or
Be able to love soulfully?

You have thousands of soul mates.
They appear as your children, parents, friends, lovers and spouses.
They appear as those you hate and those you love.
They appear in order to evolve your soul, and when their part is done
They may choose to leave or stay.

There is no guarantee that any of them
Will be your ideal life partner or
Will live with you happily ever after."

"The greatest lesson that Love teaches is

To Love for Love's sake,

To ask for nothing except Love,

To expect nothing except Love.

Love grows endlessly,

Never counting the cost of giving,

Never minding the outcome of loving.

Love's truest desire is only to Love and be loved,

To fill your beloved with Love and then overflow,

Filling all who come to you with even more Love."

"Love sees not

The banks it overflowed,

The traditions it broke,

Nor the havoc it wrought

Along its path.

Like a river rising and expanding endlessly,

Love carries all who dive into Her depths

Back to Source:

The vast endless ocean of Love

From where life's journeys began."

"The river of Love flows not for the weak hearted
Who seek safety, security and comfort.

Love makes no promises, gives no reassurances or guarantees.
Love stirs up passion in the heart and fills the soul
With longing to soar to the highest heights!

At the same time Love mercilessly exposes your weaknesses,
Rips open your carefully constructed masks and
Dismantles your well defended ego.

All that you think you are turns inside out
As Love playfully weaves Her magic spell."

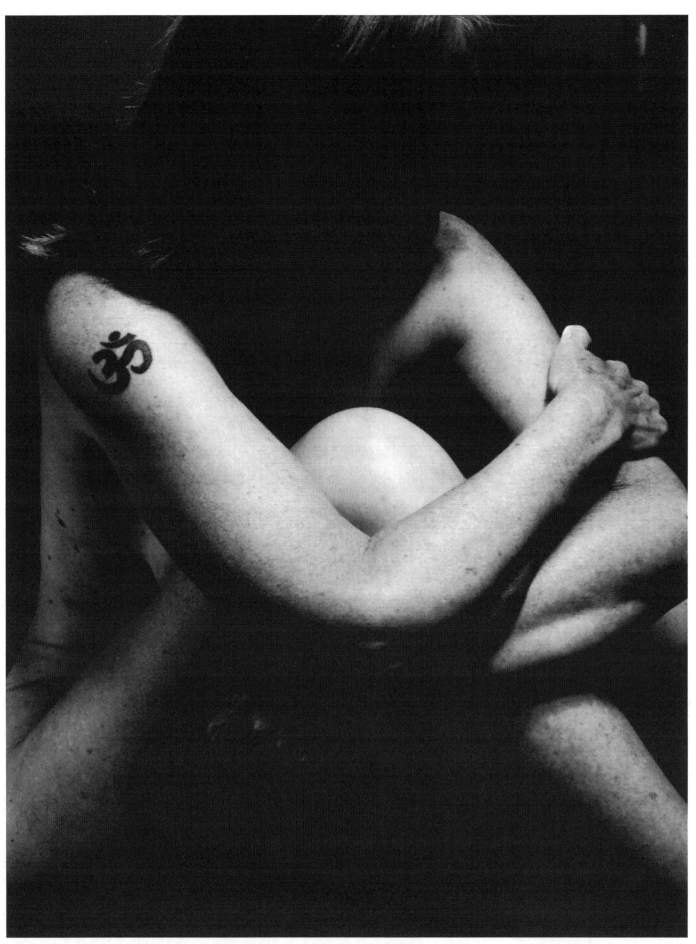

Loving Soulfully

"Love is not a destination
That once reached will allow you to rest.
Love is a journey
That will take the rest from your life.

You will not know what hit you,
Where you are going, or
What will happen next.

Love is energy in motion,
The Divine in ecstasy,
The Universe re-birthing itself --

Transforming your beloveds and you
Into Goddesses and Gods."

"Love is life: heightened, deepened and enhanced!
In Her arms you will find all that you desire
And more than you ever imagined.

Love creates and destroys,
Gives and takes away,
Fulfills yet leaves you longing for more.

It is easy to fall in love.
But those who flow with Love
Ride Her passionate waves,
Embrace Her bittersweet joys and sorrows,
Reinvent themselves relentlessly, and
Surrender everything --

They experience the highest ecstasy of Love.
They emerge enlightened, radiant, joyful and free.
They become Soulful Lovers."

Loving Soulfully

"Love calls you to:

Let loose your hesitation

That you may let go of your egoic self;

Release everything you think you are

That you may align yourself with the Soul of Love;

Dive fearlessly into Her waters

That you may arise in Love as the Beloved;

Awaken the depths of your Being

That you may reconnect with your essence as Love."

Chapter 1: I Am Love

"Wherever you find Love, follow Her fragrance

Without worrying or questioning where She is leading you.

Let Love's alluring incense captivate and transport you

Into the mysteries of your heart and soul.

Do not try to own or control Love

For She never can be yours

Instead, delight in Her effervescence,

Dance to her rhythm,

Surrender to Her flow.

Set Love free to roam the wilderness of your soul.

Let Love's mystique enthrall your being

And fill your heart with rapturous delight."

Loving Soulfully

"Love annihilates the egoic self; Her devastation is total!

You have no choice except to dive deep
Into Her luscious waters and
Inhale Her invigorating aroma
Into every cell of your being.

When the waves of Love find their energy reflected in another
They melt and merge into each other.
Then neither you nor your beloved remain.

The alchemy is complete and
All that exists is Love sweet Love."

"All that begins must end, and
All that ends must begin again.

Know that life will end,
Yet live with all your passion!
Know that relationships will end,
Yet Love with all your being!

No one knows the outcome of loving.
No one knows how Love's story will unfold.
Yet, those who dive into Her uncharted waters
Shall live to tell the tale of Her endless glory.

Love's journey takes you past the illusions of fear --
Inviting you to experience
Her potent magic,
Her enchanting presence,
Her infinite mystery."

"Love rules!

Not in the land of rules and rulers.
Not amidst those who use Her to conquer, control and dominate.

Love thrives in the hearts of the free
Who live each moment without past or future;
Who honor, admire and cherish each other;
Who worship, serve and surrender to each other.

When you open to Love
God enters through the doorway of your heart,
Transforming your world.

The egoic self makes love with the Divine and vanishes.
The illusion of separation between human and God dissolves.

Heaven dances in every cell of your being, and
Only Love remains to witness Her splendor."

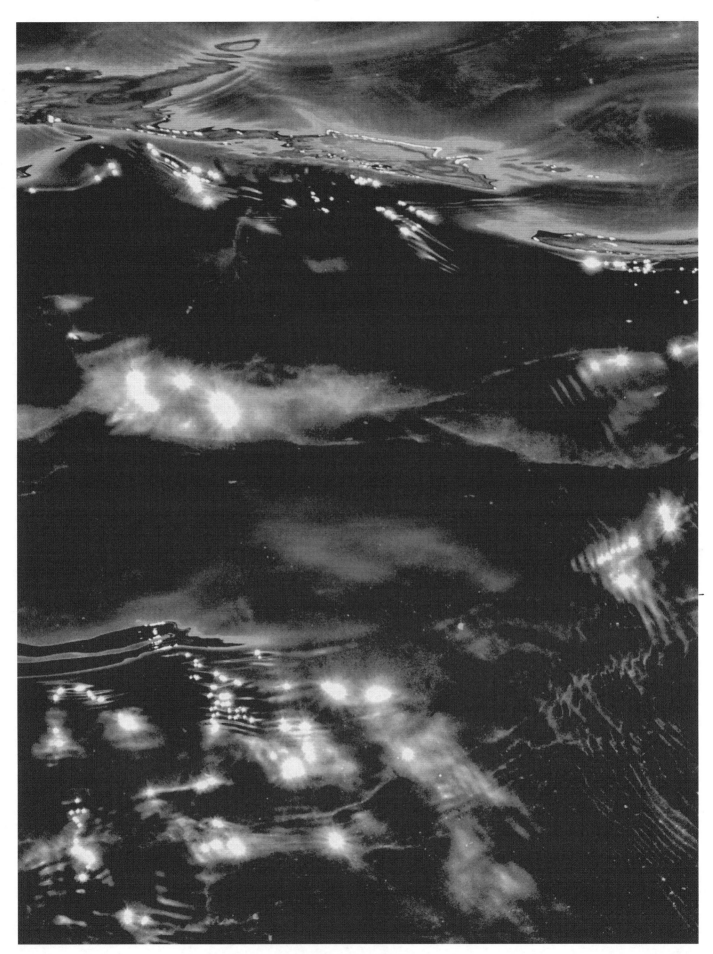

"Love has no limits, boundaries or conditions!

If you dare to enter Her Temple

She will take everything you are and

All that you have until nothing remains

Except Love -- Love -- and still more Love.

This Love never dies, is never lost, and cannot be taken away.

For She has become you, and you have become

An expression of Her primal truth, beauty and magnificence!"

Loving Soulfully

"The Source of All, the Supreme Lover, the One True Love
Wants all to be loved deeply, intimately, and endlessly.

Let everyone plunder Love's abundance;
Let all who come fill their hearts
With Her sweet treasures.

In the Kingdom of Love:

All are worthy,
All are deserving,
All are welcome.

None shall lack,
None shall be turned away,
None shall be lonely or sad."

Chapter 3: Love Is ...

Love is God

"Love is ...
The Universe experiencing itself,
The Beloved wooing itself,
The Divine communing with Its Essence
Through the hearts, eyes and bodies of lovers.

Love is ...
God enjoying the unique melody of your beloveds --
Savoring their souls, relishing their beauty,
Arousing their passion,
Making love to them through you.

Love is ...
The Source of all that is --
Adoring, worshiping and making love to you
Through endless lovers across infinity.

Behold Love's delightful magnificence"

Love is the "One"

"No one can be your 'one true love.'

No one can complete or fulfill you.

No one can be the right one for you.

The one you seek is the Source of all --

The One True Love who will

Never forsake you,

Never hurt you,

Never break your heart.

Seek not the one, who will be all and everything for you.

Seek instead to love:

The One within yourself,

The One in those you hold dear,

The One in everyone.

Love the One in all and the All in one."

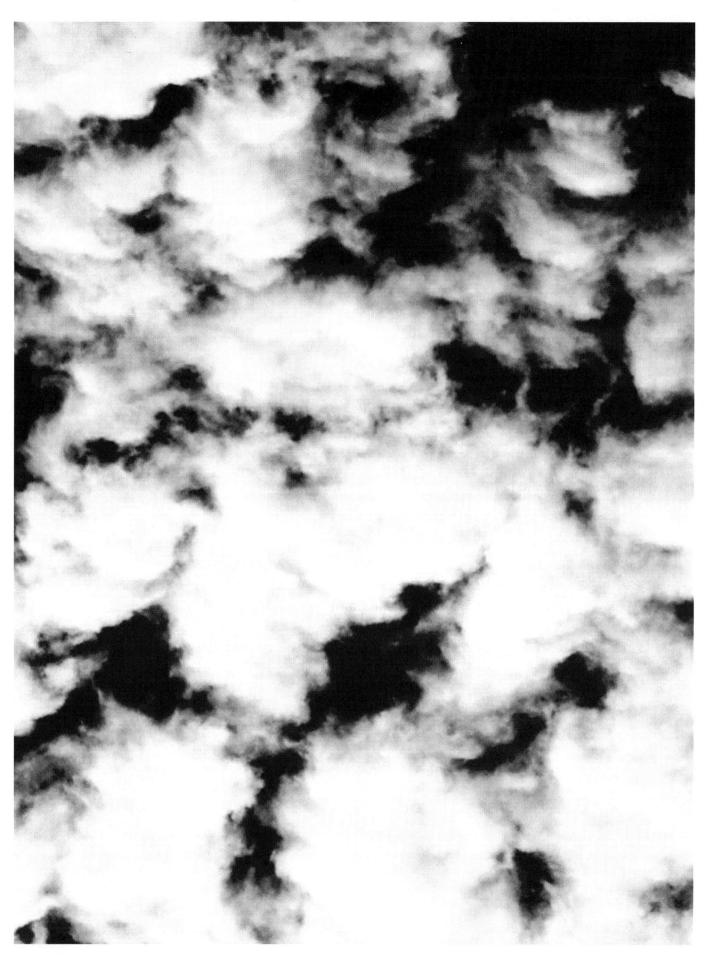

Love is Abundant

"Love longs to break free from the prison walls of
Rules, conditions, emotions, rituals, religious and social institu-
tions
That have stifled Her for thousands of years.

Love is free like the wind, abundant like the air
And resplendent like the sun!
Love is all around you, in everything and everyone.

Like the wind Love caresses every part of your body.
Like the air She infuses every cell of being.

Breathe Her delightful energy into you.
Fill yourself with Her ambrosial presence.

Allow yourself to soar on the currents of infinite Love.
Allow Her to take you to places you have never imagined!"

Loving Soulfully

Love Is Who You Are

"Make Love with everything and everyone.

Make Love with your eyes, nose, ears, words and touch.

Make Love with your mind, heart and body.

Make Love with everything you do.

Make Love your God, your religion and your meditation.

Make Love your priority, life purpose and reason for living.

Make Love your inspiration, ecstasy and passion.

Make Love your greatest possession.

Make Love your true identity.

Become a lover of Love.

Merge completely with Love.

Let nothing stand between Her and you.

In Love's eyes you will find Paradise.

In Her loving arms you will enter the 'Kingdom of Heaven.'

In Her kisses you will be One with God."

Loving Soulfully

Love is Presence

"Presence reveals Love!

When you are in the present moment with anything or anyone
You instantly experience peace, joy and Love.

When you are present to the ones you love then
You will see, hear and feel all that is wonderful in your beloveds.

Your heart will open in delight.
Your eyes will see them as divine.
Your words will be prayers of glorification.
Your actions will become offerings on the altar of Love.

Sensuality heightens presence.
Intimacy deepens sensuality.
Adoration enhances intimacy.

Love invites you:
To play with Her Energy consciously;
To create and let go, do and undo, feel and release.

Love challenges you:
To live in the moment;
To let go of disappointment and hurt;
To release the stories of the past and promises of the future;
To start each day afresh --

As if you just met,
As if now is all you have,
As if nothing matters --

Except to love and be loved."

Love Transforms

"Love is not something that just happens.

It is a creation, an expression --

A process of birthing that is both painful and joyous,

A manifestation that is both chaotic and ecstatic,

An occurrence that is unpredictable and incomprehensible.

Love's touch transforms the world

Inside you and all around you."

Love is Timeless

"Love has no future and no past.

Love has no agenda and no goal.

Love has no beginning or end.

Love is born in timelessness and thrives in freedom.

Love is blind, foolish, senseless, meaningless and has no logic or reason.

Love seeks a deep connection and intimacy with the soul of the beloved.

Love longs to dive into the arms of the beloved and lose Herself.

In losing that which cannot be lost,

Love reconnects you with your essence,

That you may find Her timeless presence within you always.

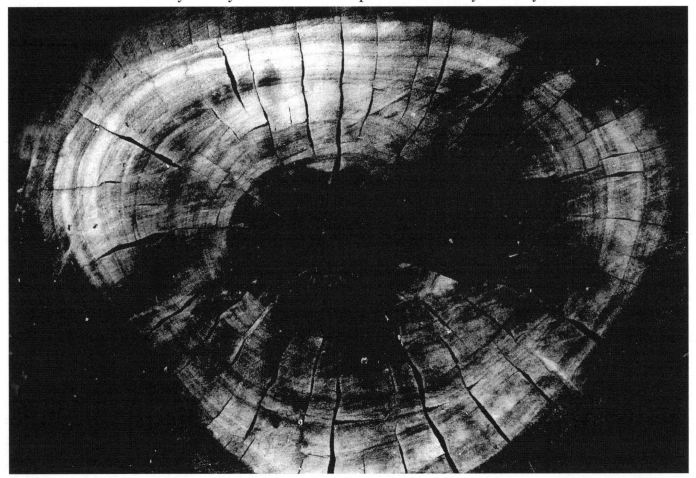

Whenever, wherever and with whomever

You open to Love, there shall you experience

Foreverness...timelessness...the infinite now.

Love connects you deeply,

Takes you on many journeys

Through the skies of time.

The Love you experience is never lost.

Lovers reconnect in many lifetimes;

Growing in love, healing wounds, expanding awareness.

When one lover leaves, another finds you.

When one journey ends another begins.

You cannot lock yourself up and hide;

Love will find you wherever you are.

The only way out is in

To the hands of Love:

To play on Love's terms,

To dance Love's tune,

To breathe Love's Essence

And become One with Love."

Loving Soulfully

Love is Formless

"Love's sacred Energy has no form --
Yet She incarnates in your world life after life;
Changing bodies, faces and personalities.

Some loved ones stay a life time while others vanish after a brief visit;
Some deepen in love while others wound and scar you.

Love does not ask you to suffer or tolerate that which is not love.
You are always at choice to be honored or abused,
To be cherished or taken for granted, to stay or leave.

What you create with Love's Energy is your responsibility.
Do not blame your lover or Love
For that which you willingly co-created.

Love comes to you in Her pure Essence
Bringing joy, ecstasy and delight.
Love bends, flows and adapts to your will.
But when misused, She moves on."

Loving Soulfully

Love is Dynamic

"The kaleidoscope of Love playfully rearranges lovers' dynamics,

Changing the cosmology of their relationships over lifetimes.

Friends, lovers, children and enemies interchange roles

As Love attracts and reunites them.

Those who define themselves by their roles

Find themselves hurting and alone.

Their rigidity robs them of the freedom

To experience Love's dynamic nature.

Soulful lovers fluidly change roles moment to moment;

Their connections have no name, no form, no rules and no structure.

They play and dance with Love's delusions.

They surrender to Love's calling and bow to her whims.

They let Love use them and be amused by them.

They allow Love to change and transform them.

They become puppets in the hands of Love."

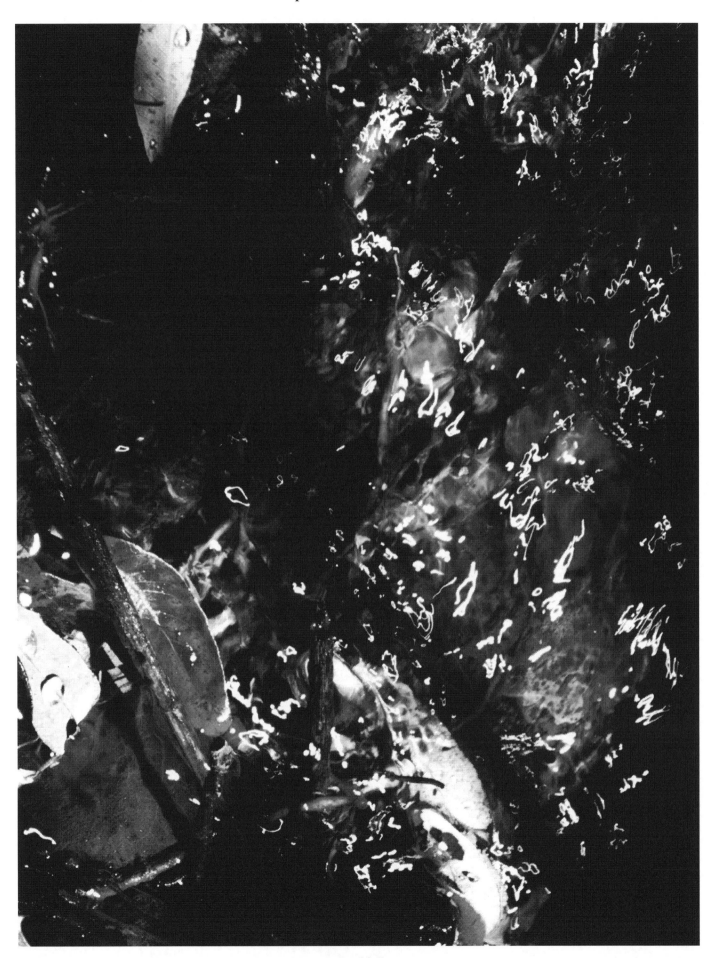

Love is Perfection

"The elusive ideal that you will find a perfect person
And live happily ever after
Sounds enticing yet inevitably leads to
Unhappiness, frustration and loneliness.

The egoic mind wants to believe that love can be found in
A perfectly shaped, attired or accomplished person.
Time shatters these illusions
As external attributes fade and wither,
As faults and imperfections become magnified,
Challenging the authenticity of that which you called love.

Love's greatest power lies in her ability:
To reveal the beauty, the uniqueness, the perfection
That lie hidden behind all perceived imperfections and flaws;
To magnify and glorify all that is delightful in the beloved,
While embracing seeming inadequacies
As sacred expressions of an evolving Universe.

Love's greatest alchemy lies in her expertise
To transform everything and everyone into Her perfect likeness.

Where you see perfection, there will you find Love.
When you see perfection in everything and everyone,
You will find Love everywhere.

Love is the perfection you seek.
Love is perfection revealed.
Love is perfection made manifest!"

Rohit Juneja

Love is Not Attraction

"Attraction arises in the egoic mind;

Fabricated by the imagination.

Like a computer algorithm it seeks someone:

Similar, to mirror you;

Different, to complete you;

Beautiful, to make you look good;

Sensitive, to understand you;

Powerful, to protect you;

Wealthy, to take care of you.

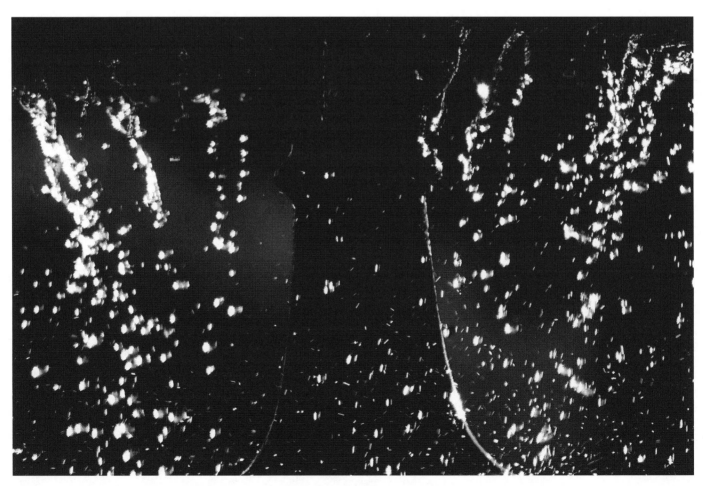

When the mind finds its Prince Charming

It is overjoyed.

It obsesses, clings and sees only that which it desires.

It strives to spin a safe, secure and permanent web.

The egoic mind expertly weaves fairy tales, assumptions and illusions.

When its expectations are not met it creates drama.

It fights, argues, blames, withdraws, weeps and defends itself.

When your lover leaves, the mind is deeply hurt, wounded and devastated.

It believes you are unworthy, undeserving and unattractive.

It believes that no one will ever love you

And that you will always be alone.

Such are the ways of unconscious egoic love.

They rarely work, barely satisfy and seldom last.

Be attracted instead to Love's unique expression in everyone.

Surround yourself with those who have similar vibrational energy.

Allow yourself to be seen, cherished and adored.

Love deeply, completely, passionately and fearlessly.

Let your cup overflow endlessly."

Loving Soulfully

Love Does not "Fall In Love"

"'Falling in love' is an ideal based on scarcity.
The ideal lover is hard to find, harder to keep and hardest to let go.

You hope to stumble upon the 'one,' magically fulfilling your wish list.
Yet in reality the criteria that define your ideal lover filter out Love,
Leaving you feeling unfulfilled and isolated.

'Rising in Love' is abundant, frequent and limitless.
There is no need to control and hold on.
There is no fear of letting go and moving on.

Love presents an endless stream of lovers --
Each expressing Her mystery,
Evoking unique aspects of yourself,
Mirroring in endless prisms the beauty of who you really are. Choose not
the form that Love must take
Based on some list of egoic criteria.

As a master potter allows the clay to find its own shape,
Let Love sculpt her own form and find
Her authentic expression with each lover.

True Love comes --
When you are true to Love.
When you put aside your egoic ideals and surrender to Her will.
When you let Love uplift your consciousness and ignite your spirit.
When you know without a doubt that you are deathless.
When you live as if this is your last moment on earth.
When you love with the awareness
That Love is all that truly matters."

Rohit Juneja

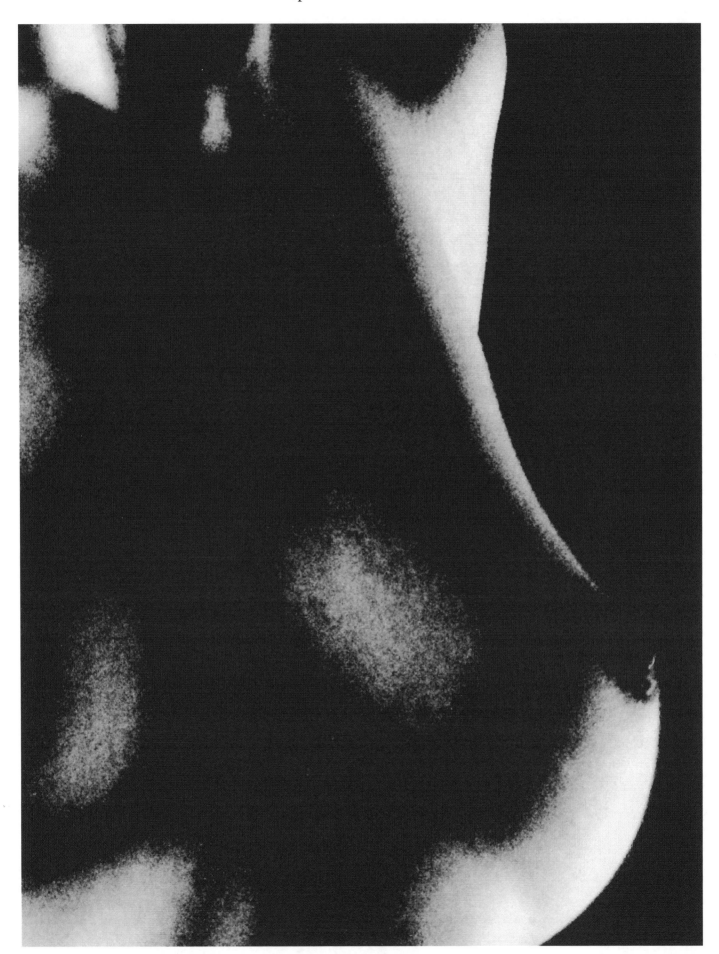

Loving Soulfully

Love Will Not Complete You

"What you have not valued in yourself
You will find attractive in another.

What you treasure in another
Already lies hidden within you.

Delight in your exquisite self.
Love and romance yourself.
Be full, complete and at peace with yourself.

Let the abundant fountain of Love within you overflow,
Showering all who come to you
With Love's delightful nectar."

Loving Soulfully

Love Has No Expectations

"When you bring expectations, needs and fears to the Temple of Love

They will stand as boulders that contaminate Love with their heaviness.

They will pound your precious heart to pulp, leaving you sad and bewildered.

The baggage you bring to Love must be abandoned at Her doorstep.

For Love comes:

Not to serve you, but to be served;

Not to please you, but to be pleased;

Not to fulfill you, but to connect you with yourself;

Not to be abused by you, but to dissolve all that you think you are.

Love expects nothing but takes everything.

Love strips you naked, makes you vulnerable,

And gives nothing in return except Love."

Loving Soulfully

Love Has No Need

"Those who go to Love to fulfill their needs
Must pay the price of Love in exchange.

Love will not allow Herself to be used by you.
Love's intent is to use you to express Herself.

When you resist Love's intent She vanishes,
Leaving you with shadows and memories.

The ones you use to fulfill your needs
Have needs of their own.
In the battlefield of needs,
Many have found themselves battered and alone.

Seek not another to fulfill your needs.
All that you need, desire and seek lies within you.
You are complete and powerful in your Self.

Marvel at the tapestry of your exquisiteness.
Explore its intriguing occurrence in another.

Then you will know the secret of the divine paradox:
You are all One yet different, Divine yet human,
Perfect yet imperfect, complete yet wanting more.

Then you will know that there is nothing you need, yet
Love is all you will ever need."

Loving Soulfully

Love Has No Purpose

"Love has no goal.

Love is complete in itself.

Love is its own purpose.

Love's deepest desire is to love and be loved.

As Love moves through you She heals life's wounds --

Giving you courage to push through your limitations, judgments and fears;

Opening your heart and expanding your consciousness.

Love transforms everyone She touches into Love --

With rapture, fascination, ecstasy and passion;

With beauty, music, poetry, dance and romance;

With worship, reverence, devotion and surrender.

Love animates your spirit --

Inviting you to experience the divine within and without,

Transforming struggle into ease,

Pain into pleasure,

And suffering into comfort."

Loving Soulfully

Love Does Not Mind

"The egoic mind is frail and fearful,

Unable to grasp the true nature of Love.

It constructs walls, ideals and norms to hold on to Love.

It concocts conditions, fears and mistrust to control Love.

It exploits religion, society and tradition to regulate Love.

The trickster mind contaminates Love.

It twists your thoughts, bewilders your emotions;

It manufactures all manner of untruths;

It doubts your lover, creates imaginary scenarios and incites conflict.

Sooner or later Love finds a way:

To liberate Herself from the mind's control,

To tunnel through the corridors of your soul,

To break free from confining relationships,

And breathe the fresh air of Her natural sweetness.

Mind and Love are polarities that rarely meet.

When you mind you will not Love and

When you Love you will not mind."

Love is Simple

"When you are in the arms of Love --
You will smile more often,
Be happy for no reason,
Enjoy the smallest pleasures and
Find ecstasy in ordinary things.

Love is simple, beautiful and joyful.
The mind is complex and distorts
Thoughts, emotions and relationships.

To perfect the art of Love --
You must also perfect the art
Of not thinking,
Of being in the moment,
Of discovering the extraordinary in the ordinary."

Loving Soulfully

Love is Playful

"If you want Love to stay with you eternally,

Keep Her away from the shadow of:

Social, religious and cultural norms;

Expectations, needs and fears;

Rules, roles and routines;

Logic, reason and sensibility.

Love delights in celebrating existence playfully.

Love thrives in the sunshine of

Spontaneity, imagination and creativity --

Where She can dance joyfully,

Expand possibilities,

Create change,

Explore variety and

Break through limitations."

Love is Constantly Changing

"Love's journey is filled with change and uncertainty.

The way you love is never static.
The one you love changes over time.
You, too, grow and evolve over time.

Love has a life of Its own,
Morphing through stages that feel like
Youth, adulthood, old age, death and reincarnation.

Those who resist Love's dynamic ways
Find themselves entrenched in resentment, bitterness and loneliness.
They become fearful of Love, armor their hearts
And relive their sad stories.

Love is never lost, never wasted and is never a failure.
Each lover is a playground for Love's expression.
Each relationship births a new version of yourself.

Each separation is the gift of a clean slate,
Manifesting an even greater expression of who you really are,
Expanding your heart to receive even more Love.

Love invites you to
Burn the memories of your tumultuous past and
Throw off the protective layers that isolate you.

Sail Her stormy seas and trust Her expert navigation
As She shows you how to be truly alive and live from the heart."

Rohit Juneja

Loving Soulfully

Love is Unique

"Love comes on Her own inexplicable terms.
Each time She appears is unlike any other.
Each time She unveils another facet of
Her unique qualities, rhythm and flow.

No lover is like another.
No lover can ever replace another.
No love affair is better than another.

All are fascinating and special in their own way.
All are unique expressions of Love's infinite poetry.

Stay grounded in this knowing and
Jealousy will skim by you.
Stay rooted in your own specialness and
Love will thrive in your heart."

Loving Soulfully

Love is Unconditional

"Love honors you as you are and
Trusts you unconditionally.

In Her adoring eyes you can do no wrong.
All that you did and will ever do is part of Her fascinating story.
Your mistakes are welcome.
Your blunders are necessary.
Through them Love shows you
How unflinchingly She cherishes you.

In Love's infinite wisdom there is no duality --
No good or bad, right or wrong, saint or sinner, better or worse.

All are equal, beautiful and divine sparks.
All are adorable, precious and exquisite.
All are radiant manifestations of the Divine.

When you Love unconditionally
You experience what your soul has always desired:
To be One with Love,
To be Love."

Love is Surrender

"Love welcomes everyone --
Alluring you with Her seductive charms,
Breaking your protective walls,
Stealing your precious mind,
Enticing you do things you would not ordinarily do,
Making you drunk with Her ecstatic Energy.

No one is more or less deserving of Love's abundance.
No one is worthy or unworthy.
No one is better or worse.

In surrendering to Love there are no winners or losers.
Love takes all of yourself and gives all of Herself --
Enriching, enlightening and expanding you.

In surrendering everything to Love you become nothing.
In nothingness Love carves you in Her likeness.

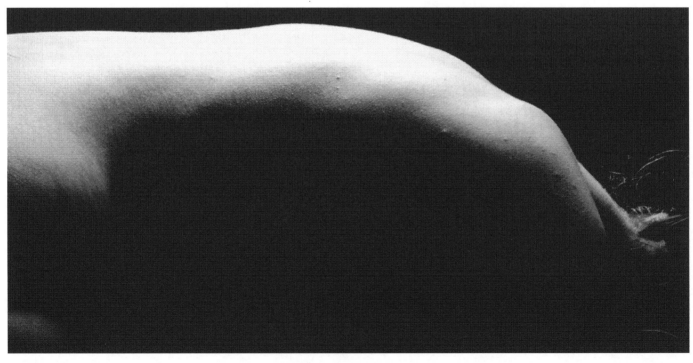

In exchange for your surrender Love will not reward you with
Security, safety, comfort, happiness or permanence.

Love will not thank you or validate you.
Nor will She keep track of what you did or did not do.

Love's doors are not open for barter or accounting;
Nor does She give any assurance of fairness, equality or justice.

Leave these egoic ideals
Outside the Temple of Love.

Enter empty handed --
Ready to die at any moment;
Ready to lose your mind, ego and self;
Ready to forsake your nationality, religion and identity;
Ready to trust Love's skillful carving hand;

As She deepens the chalice of your heart,
Enhancing its capacity to give and receive Love."

Loving Soulfully

Love is Worship

"Worship your soul and you will worship God.
Worship each other and you will be God.

Worship Love
By cherishing, adoring and bowing;
By surrendering body, mind and soul.

When Love is worshipped, then --
Love becomes your meditation,
Love becomes your prayer,
Love becomes your deity,
Love becomes your existence.

Then Love is all there is!"

Loving Soulfully

Love is Prayer

"Love's prayer arises from a place of fullness,
Overflowing from one lover to another.

Love magnifies and glorifies all that is delightful in the beloved,
While embracing and adoring flaws and imperfections as
Sacred expressions of an evolving Universe.

Love expresses Her prayer by serving the beloved
With heartfelt humility,
With selfless giving,
With utmost surrender.

Love's prayer is not a one way street --
Where one receives and the other gives,
Where one is great and the other small.

In the Temple of Love
God worships you, glorifies you, serves you, and surrenders to you.
Here lover and beloved, God and human, unite as One."

Love is Intimate

"Intimacy unites heaven and Earth.

The deeper you dive into your beloved,
The more you relish each other's body, mind and soul --
The more you will discover the Goddess and God in each other.

Love is the religion of God.

Adoration is the prayer that opens the heart.
Sensuality is the meditation that invites God.
Romance is the foreplay that arouses God.
Orgasm is the ecstasy that incarnates God.
Love is the doorway to Oneness with God.

The bed you make love on is
The most sacred spot on Earth;
The ultimate Church or Temple of the Divine.

The body is the altar on which God
Awakens your passion for divine pleasure,
Worships your beloved and you,
Consummates your desire through sacred orgasm.

In the sacred union of your beings
God dances to the rhythm of your orgasmic bliss;
Giving birth to aliveness, ecstasy, inspiration and creativity.

Pay no attention to the impostors who distort God in the name of religion.

They shame, suppress and demonize your sexuality through their blind faith.

Strip off the shackles and set yourself free.

Break the limitations, the conditions and the social norms.

Be shameless, fearless and guiltless.

Give yourself permission to --

Celebrate your body,

Heighten your desire,

Deepen your pleasure,

Enhance your ecstasy.

Savor each other sensually.

Relish each other's presence.

Bask in each other's beauty.

Nourish each other with tender loving care.

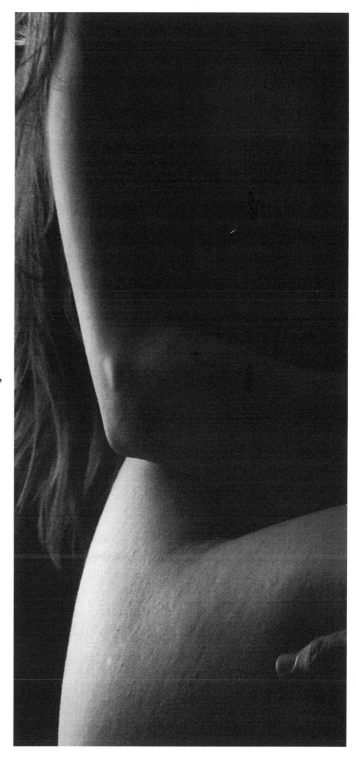

Sex is the primal creative energy of the Universe,

The source of life and the Essence of Source.

You were born from sex,

Are enlivened by sex,

And wither without sex.

Celebrate your sexuality!

Enjoy as much sex and pleasure as you desire.

Sex and spirit cannot be separated for

God is sex and sex is Divine."

Loving Soulfully

Love is For Giving

"Love dies in fear and withers when controlled.

Love thrives in freedom and multiplies when given freely.

Set Love free!

Share Her with everyone you meet.

The more you give Love,

The more She will flow through you and fill you.

The less you discriminate, manipulate or hold on to Love,

The more She will be your constant companion.

Giving Love does not mean giving your heart or your self to another.

Your Self is a gift from Source that is not to be given.

In giving yourself away you diminish your light --

That which was most lovable about you.

Then nothing remains: not you, your beloved, nor Love.

Be neither the giver nor the receiver of Love,

Be the conduit through which Love flows.

Allow Love's Energy to embody you.

Let Love express Herself through you.

Receive Her from your beloved

And with deepest gratitude offer Love back to Herself."

Love is Free

"Love is a free spirit that comes and goes as it chooses.

Love is constant, yet always evolving.

Love is forever, yet does not strive to bind you to each other.

Love possesses you, yet the one you love never can be owned or possessed.

The one you own will imprison you.

The one you possess will consume you.

Love despises these prison walls of attachment,

And dies to set Herself free to roam the vast skies of possibility.

Loving Soulfully

Chapter 3: Love Is ...

Love is not currency with which you can
Purchase another's heart "until death do you part."

You cannot own or possess anyone.
Nor can Love be found in being possessed by another.

You came into this world alone and will die alone.
The egoic mind perceives this aloneness as loneliness
And longs to be with someone forever.

Those who embrace this aloneness experience Divine connection
Wherein lies the key to lasting peace, fulfillment, joy and Love.

Vows cannot insure undying love.
You cannot manipulate or bargain with Love.
Your fears and insecurities cannot entice Love to stay.

Love in Her truest form never dies.
Yet, when you bind Love She vanishes gradually.
Suddenly, you find yourself surrounded by
Complacency, routine, boredom and lack of desire;
Pain, sorrow, loneliness, loss and grief.
Shake off your fears and insecurities.
Set your beloved and yourself free
Without trying to possess or control
That which never can be yours.

The spirit of Love is free as the wind,
Limitless as the sky and
Abundant as the Universe.

Love Love as She desires to be loved
And She will be yours forever."

Rohit Juneja

Love is Expansive

"Love challenges you constantly to

Expand your capacity to love.

Those who Love conditionally often pay a heavy price.

The passion and exuberance they once had die away.

What you experience as adultery and affairs

Are Love's attempts to rekindle the excitement of new relationships

And spurn the imprisonment of puritanical codes and religious edicts.

Rules may be used to suppress Love's expansion,

Yet Love refuses to be limited in any way.

That which is expansive must break free!

Love will have Her way, regardless.

Adulterated Love leads to adultery.

Lovers cheat, deceive and lie

Not because they are bad or untrustworthy

But because they do not trust themselves or Love.

Love has Her own ethics, integrity and truth.

Her path is one of unshakeable and implicit trust.

Love trusts you to be true to yourself,

To follow your heart,

To explore new possibilities

That will enrich your experience of life.

Love uplifts Soulful Lovers to a dimension

Beyond jealousy, insecurity or fear.

Loving Soulfully

Love loves to Love for Love's sake.

Love wants you to be in love over and over again.

Love has no reason, discrimination, discernment or judgment.

You cannot restrict or limit Love through

Vows of fidelity, monogamy or marriage

That will tie Her down and make Her yours.

Love gives no assurances,

Nor adheres to agreements, contracts or promises.

Know Love's true nature;

Honor Her and She will be yours forever.

Resist her nature and you will keep losing her forever.

The choice is yours!

Love wants you to rise in Love --

With Love,

With God,

With life,

With everyone,

With all that is."

Love is Not Safe

"The boundaries that keep you safe
Are the prisons that limit your horizons.

Boundaries can be useful at times
But may trap you in their neurotic web of never ending deceit.

Safety and security attract the egoic mind
But are likely to suppress your deepest longings.

The more you strive to be safe
The more you lose your essence and Love.

Death is safe and free of risk, yet you fear it.
Life is unsafe and insecure, yet you refuse to embrace it.
In rejecting these truths you negate living.

To be safe is to agree to a living death!
You have bargained with the "Devil"
And wonder why your life is a living "Hell."

Through your attempt to control a world that cannot be controlled
You die to life's myriad expressions,
Her infinite mysteries and unparalleled joys!

Love is life fully expressed.

Love is vibrant, pulsating and dynamic:

Filled with risks, fears and unknown mysteries;

Filled with challenges, upheavals and chaos.

Love brings you to the edge of fear,

Pushes you over the cliff of safety,

That you may be your truest Self,

Experience life's most delectable delights

And soar Her infinite galaxies."

Loving Soulfully

Love is Fearless

"Cast aside the fear filled ways of egoic love.

They isolate you from each other,

Leaving you sad, lonely and afraid.

Fear disintegrates Love.

Fearlessness enhances Love.

The belief that love is limited and conditional,

That there is one special love meant just for you,

Makes love the nightmare it has become.

Realize beyond any doubt that --

Love is the Divine loving you,

Love is energy that cannot be created or destroyed,

It always was, is and will be with you.

Then you will experience

Love that does not hurt, Love that is with you always.

You will become fearless lovers --

Ready to dive into the deepest waters of Love,

Ready to rise to Love's highest heights,

Ready to take on Love's toughest challenges,

Ready to experience Love's greatest ecstasies.

To know such Love is the purest quest of all,

The Holy Grail that will unite all as One."

Love is Eternal

"As day appears to be vanquished by night,

So it appears that romantic love dies,

Leaving you heartbroken and alone.

Yet Love has no beginning or end;

Love neither dies nor is She ever born.

Love is with you eternally.

At times Love comes to you through one lover,

Then leaves and reappears through another and then another.

At times Love comes through many lovers simultaneously,

Inviting you to open your heart to even more Love.

Love reminds you constantly of Her presence

Appearing through loved ones, pets, children or even strangers.

Forms change, people come and go.

But Love's Energy and Essence are ever present.

Loving Soulfully

Love appears and disappears like waves.

It is pointless to lament the loss of a wave.

Waves cannot be held or possessed.

They must be free to rise, fall and merge into the ocean of Love

To arise again, as new waves, new forms, new expressions of Love.

Each new expression fills your life with joy, makes your soul sing

And awakens your heart to Divine Love.

Love never leaves.

God reaches out infinitely,

Loving you through all your beloveds

Life after life."

Rohit Juneja

Love Does Not Hurt

"It is not Love that hurts,

But rather what you do with Love.

When you distort Love and make it

That which you want,

That which it is not,

Then you wound yourself and each other!

When loved ones betray, hurt, leave or disappoint you,

Thank them for having exposed the lie.

They have shown you how flawed, fragile and pathetic romantic love was.

Break your heart; it is the best thing you will ever do!

The shell of the egoic heart is made up of

Emotional wounds from thousands of lifetimes.

Rip your heart wide open, tear away its limitations

Until nothing remains of its story of victimization.

Let go your resistance, fear and doubt.

Let go your attachment to pain and suffering.

Welcome falling that you may fly,

Losing that you may win,

Dying that you may live.

Then invite your soul to teach you

The dance of Divine Love --

The path to rising in love

And loving soulfully."

Rohit Juneja

Chapter 4: Loving Soulfully

Inspired by Love's guidance,

I resume my journey.

She reassures me:

"I shall never leave you.

I am yours and you are mine forever.

One body, one mind, one soul,

One heart, one Universe, one Love --

Dancing together through eternity.

May you find Love everywhere.

May Love's enthralling presence be with you always.

May you be filled with --

The light of delight,

The touch of ecstatic pleasure,

The whisper of inspiration."

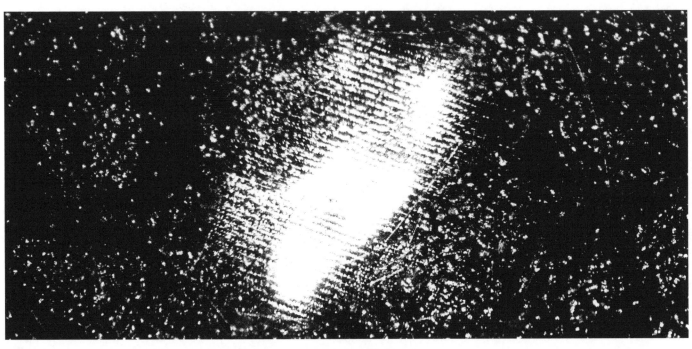

I walk Love's path --

I live Her dream.

I let go of my story,

I stop struggling to be safe and secure.

I find myself --

Embracing life in all its colors,

Feeling more alive than ever.

I Love who I am.

Love shows me --

That I am perfect with all my flaws,

That life is wonderful no matter what happens,

That no one can harm or hurt me except me.

I realize that --

I am free to be authentically me,

I am free to love and be loved endlessly.

Stillness takes me into the depths of my Soul.

My heart opens like a flower.

Within its delicate petals,

I find the Source of Love --

The key to loving soulfully, fearlessly and uninhibitedly;

The secret to being Love and rising in Love;

The yearning to share this blessed Love with everyone.

It was inside me all along.

Now I see that you have it too.

You are me and I am you.

In loving you I discover me.

In loving myself I manifest you.

Our reflections in each other

Stretch like mirrors into infinity.

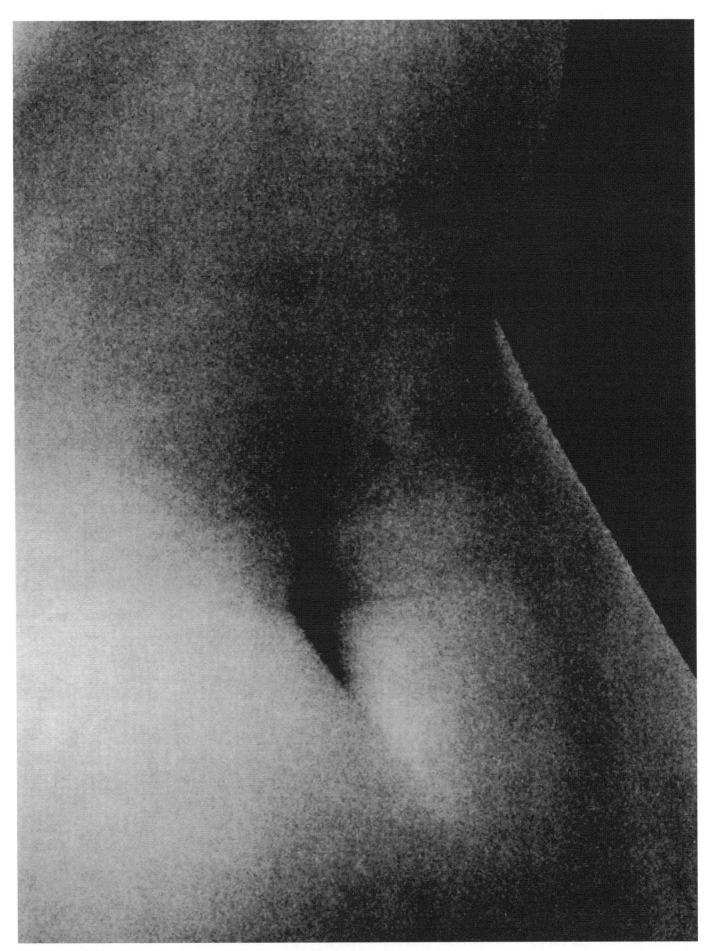

Loving Soulfully

I am in Love!

Not with a person but

With everyone, everything and nothing.

I feel this Love

In me, around me, surrounding me, becoming me.

My thoughts were clouding my world.

Now the clouds have vanished.

I can see clearly:

Love was always there but I was too preoccupied to experience it.

I am swimming in an ocean of Love.

I am in Love with Love!

I Love you! ... and you! ... and you! ... and you!

Intimately, deeply, completely, passionately, endlessly.

It does not matter whether you love me.

My heart is wide open.

I am Love unfolding, expressing, exploding.

Loving deeply without expecting or needing anything

Feels at the same time expansive yet frightening,

Freeing yet unsafe and unguarded.

I embrace my emotions with gentleness, and

Continue my journey of loving soulfully.

I see that --

Love is not a perfect person.

Love is God radiating through you and me.

Why would I want to limit Love when

We are all each others' beloved?

The Supreme Lover wants all to be loved.

Who am I to say yes to one and no to the other?

In deepest gratitude I thank you for receiving this Love.

You are all my adored, worshipped beloveds.

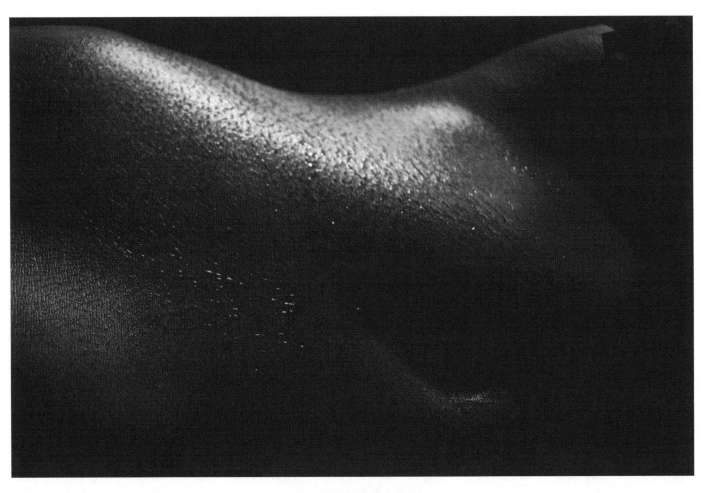

Herein lies the truth of my soul: I Love you!

This Love is formless: I feel that I am your friend, lover, partner, child, parent and soul mate. I am everything possible and impossible to you. Choose whatever form feels right for now and know that this expression of Love will evolve over time.

This Love is timeless: I feel deeply connected with you, as though we have been together for lifetimes, traveled many journeys, and our meeting was divinely arranged. Whether you choose to ignore it or accept it, this Love will be there for eternity.

This Love has no expectations: I do not expect you to feel the same way. I do not expect you to reciprocate or respond. I do not ask for you to agree or disagree. There is no particular path on which this Love must flow. It has no goal or outcome. It just is.

This Love has no need: I need nothing from you. I ask nothing; there is nothing you need to do for me. I am happy feeling what I feel. Love is sufficient unto itself.

This Love has no fear: I do not fear whether you will like me, accept me or be with me. I do not fear rejection, abandonment, loneliness or loss because I know without a doubt that Love cannot be destroyed. Love is within me always. I humbly receive this exquisite gift from Source and share Her Essence with you.

This Love is not exclusive or possessive: it is free, abundant and unlimited. There are no strings attached. There are no vows or agreements to tie you down. You are and always have been a free spirit. This Love is not a trap to take away that freedom, to own, control or manipulate you. There is no hidden agenda. Only Love!

Come with me
To enjoy Love's tantalizing flavors,
Her sensuous colors and heady aroma.

Before you enter this wondrous space
Of playful, frivolous, nowness, I invite you to --
Strip away the layers of thoughts, worries and fears;
Come naked, open, vulnerable and in your essence;
Be mindful, innocent and care free.

Find the fountain of Love within you.
Recognize Source as your primary lover.
For without that connection
You will be unable to experience soulful love.

Here your age, size, fame or fortune
Do not matter.
All that matters is --
The warmth of your heart,
Your childlike innocence,
Your surrender into the arms of Love.

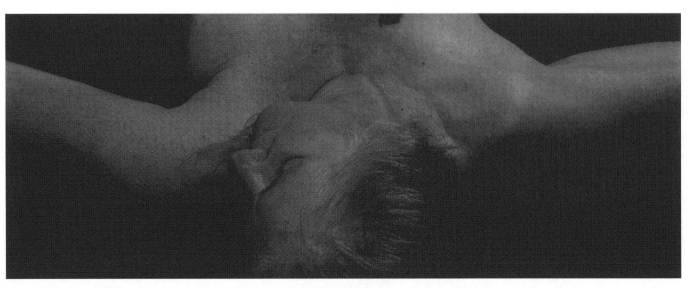

Chapter 4: Loving Soulfully

Love beckons me
To dive headlong into Her glory --
To feel Her magic,
Experience Her wildness,
Surge with Her passion.

Love awakens in the dead of night.
In darkness She shows me
What eyes cannot see and hands cannot touch.

The veil lifts, the mind quietens, senses ignite.
The world comes alive and we are lost in each other.

You look into my eyes:
You see yourself in me,
I see myself in you.

Come into my arms.
Behold the wonder of the paradise that lies
In your eyes, my breath, your whispers, my sighs.
Let us journey into forever in this moment.
Let us taste eternity here and now.

Bodies dissolve, touch intensifies, time stops.
I hold your body.
I feel your presence all around me,
Over me, under you, in me, within you.

In our infinitesimal souls we find Love's infinitude.
As we enter into the arms of the Beloved
Our separateness ceases to exist.
We feel, see, and know ourselves as One.

Rohit Juneja

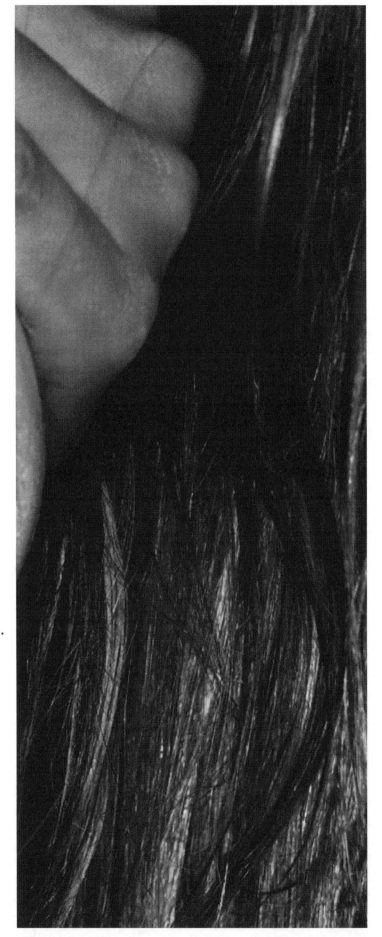

I Love you.

From the depths of my soul,
From every cell in my body.

I Love you.

One touch, one look into your eyes --
Time stops and I am in this world no more.

In loving you --
I am rejuvenated, recreated and fully alive.
I experience myself as I never have.
I am filled and fulfilled.
I am speechless.
I am in heaven.

You see me in ways I never saw myself.
You inspire me to Love myself as you Love me.

Your presence is a miracle.
I thank God, the Universe and all
Who conspired to bring us together.

I Love you eternally.

In your presence

Love carries me to a sacred world.

Our meeting feels divinely ordained

As a deep knowing of your soul arises in me.

Every moment feels timeless,

As we are together in times future and past.

My soul stands on the edge of a cliff looking to the heavens.

Joy flows like a river through the valley of my being.

The clouds dance with the gentle caress of the wind.

The sky rises to touch the sun,

As a wordless song fills my heart.

Every breath we share feels familiar yet new,

Every heartbeat surges with passion and aliveness,

As our souls quiver in euphoric union.

What is it that makes me

Fascinated when I look at you,

Electrified when I touch you?

What power is it that

Overwhelms me when we embrace,

Enthralls me when we kiss?

Looking at you is sweet torture.

In you I see God.

In you I feel all that is.

I invite you to

Become One with me,

Ravage my heart,

Ravish my body,

Infuse my bloodstream,

Tingle through my skin,

Shine within my eyes.

I want to savor you like wine.

I want to hold you, touch you, caress you.

I want to inhale you deep into my heart and soul.

Let us be drunk with Love,

See only Love,

Think only Love,

Be only Love.

Love brings a strange madness with it;

A sense that nothing exits other than Love,

That my only purpose for existence is to love and be loved.

Love makes me feel that everything is possible.

Love makes me feel powerful, invincible and adventurous.

Perhaps true sanity is --

To lose my rationality,

To give up everything for Love.

Great riches, beautiful lovers, earthly pleasures:

Nothing in this world means anything without Love.

Love melts my heart and fills my soul.

She takes me to heights I have never known.

I am a student, a witness and a puppet in Love's hands.

She bewilders, humbles and uses me.

Love delights me, uplifts me, makes me come alive.

I am mystified, amazed and awestruck by Love.

I see things as never before.

I bow before Love.

My egoic mind settles into stillness.

I feel light, peaceful and elated.

I am filled with the greatest riches and

Blessed for all eternity.

I would not trade Love for anything

In this world or any other.

I seek no greater Paradise,

No sweeter liberation and

Nothing more than to give and receive Love eternally.

In Love

I find God.

I am in Heaven,

Here and Now!

Rohit Juneja

The Love Goes On

Dearest Lover,

I hope you enjoyed reading "Loving Soulfully" as much as I enjoyed writing it. If you would like to join me in sharing this inspirational message with the world, then please:

Review: write a heart felt review and copy-paste it in the "Loving Soulfully" page on
(a) Amazon.com (b) iTunes iBookStore (c) www.facebook.com/rohit.juneja.author

Webinars, Workshops, Podcasts & Videos: lets go deeper into the mysteries of Loving Soulfully or Sacred Love, with yourself and in all your relationships. Learn how to practically live the profound wisdom in this book as I personally guide you, answer your questions and give you the practical tools you need to quiet your mind, listen to your inner voice and bring soulfulness into every aspect of your life.

To get more information please go to my website **www.RohitJuneja.com**
(a) sign up for the Newsletter (b) Go to the "Courses" tab for Webinars and Workshops (c) Go to the "Social" tab for Podcasts and Videos.

With love,
Rohit

About the Author

Rohit Juneja was born in New Delhi, grew up in Mumbai, India and currently lives in San Diego.

His lifelong search for meaning led him to explore literature, music, art, cinema, science, psychology, religion and mysticism. In Vrindavan, under the guidance of a devotional mystic, he learned to connect with Source or God and listen to the immense wisdom of his "inner voice." This awakening led to prolific writing through which he received succinct answers to all his questions and transformed his life.

Rohit is a self actualized, down to earth, modern day mystic. This means that he is deeply spiritual but does not follow any religion, doctrine or norms. He practices living with awareness, presence, gratitude and Love. At the same time he enjoys life, its pleasures, comforts and technologies.

He works as a Spiritual Counselor and Conscious Relationship Coach with people all over the world in-person and online. Through webinars, workshops and individual coaching he guides individuals and couples to experience inner peace, fulfillment, joy and self love, along with enhancing the quality of their relationships.

For more information: **www.RohitJuneja.com**

For the EBook Version of "Loving Soulfully" go to Amazon.com or iTunes iBook Store

Also by Rohit: "God You Sexy Devil" available on Amazon.com